THE BALTIMORE TWINS

A Comedy in six scenes, four dreams
And (at least) six wigs

BY
PAULA VOGEL

★

DRAMATISTS
PLAY SERVICE
INC.

THE MINEOLA TWINS
Copyright © 1999, Paula Vogel

All Rights Reserved

CAUTION: Professionals and amateurs are hereby warned that performance of THE MINEOLA TWINS is subject to payment of a royalty. It is fully protected under the copyright laws of the United States of America, and of all countries covered by the International Copyright Union (including the Dominion of Canada and the rest of the British Commonwealth), and of all countries covered by the Pan-American Copyright Convention, the Universal Copyright Convention, the Berne Convention, and of all countries with which the United States has reciprocal copyright relations. All rights, including professional/amateur stage rights, motion picture, recitation, lecturing, public reading, radio broadcasting, television, video or sound recording, all other forms of mechanical or electronic reproduction, such as CD-ROM, CD-I, DVD, information storage and retrieval systems and photocopying, and the rights of translation into foreign languages, are strictly reserved. Particular emphasis is placed upon the matter of readings, permission for which must be secured from the Author's agent in writing.

The English language stock and amateur stage performance rights in the United States, its territories, possessions and Canada for THE MINEOLA TWINS are controlled exclusively by DRAMATISTS PLAY SERVICE, INC., 440 Park Avenue South, New York, NY 10016. No professional or nonprofessional performance of the Play may be given without obtaining in advance the written permission of DRAMATISTS PLAY SERVICE, INC., and paying the requisite fee.

Inquiries concerning all other rights should be addressed to William Morris Agency, Inc., 1325 Avenue of the Americas, 15th Floor, New York, NY 10019.

SPECIAL NOTE

Anyone receiving permission to produce THE MINEOLA TWINS is required to give credit to the Author as sole and exclusive Author of the Play on the title page of all programs distributed in connection with performances of the Play and in all instances in which the title of the Play appears for purposes of advertising, publicizing or otherwise exploiting the Play and/or a production thereof. The name of the Author must appear on a separate line, in which no other name appears, immediately beneath the title and in size of type equal to 50% of the size of the largest, most prominent letter used for the title of the Play. No person, firm or entity may receive credit larger or more prominent than that accorded the Author. The following acknowledgment must appear on the title page in all programs distributed in connection with performances of the Play:

World Premiere Produced by Trinity Repertory Company, 1997.
Oskar Eustis, Artistic Director; Patricia Egan, Managing Director.

Originally developed by Perseverance Theatre, Douglas, Alaska.
This play was made possible by generous support from the Pew Charitable Trust.

SPECIAL NOTE ON SONGS AND RECORDINGS

For performances of copyrighted songs, arrangements or recordings mentioned in this Play, the permission of the copyright owner(s) must be obtained. Other songs, arrangements or recordings may be substituted provided permission from the copyright owner(s) of such songs, arrangements or recordings is obtained; or songs, arrangements or recordings in the public domain may be substituted

THE CHARACTERS

Myrna, the "Good" twin. Stacked.
Myra, played by the same actress as Myrna. The "evil" twin.
Identical to Myrna, except in the chestal area.
Jim, Myrna's fiance.
Kenny, Myrna's son.
Ben, played by the same actor as Kenny. Myra's son.
Sarah, played by an actress who also plays Jim.
Two psychiatric aides, federal agents, etc. Non-speaking characters who can also help change the furniture.

TIME

Scenes One and Two take place during the Eisenhower administration.
Scenes Three and Four take place at the beginning of the Nixon administration.
Scenes Five and Six take place during the Bush administration.
An intermission occurs after Scene Three.

PRODUCTION NOTES

There are two ways to do this play:

1. With good wigs.
2. With bad wigs.

Personally, I prefer the second way.

It would be nice to score this production with female vocalists of the period — Teresa Brewer, Doris Day, Vikki Carr, Nancy Sinatra, etc. These singers were on the Top Ten; as a country, we should never be allowed to forget this.

ABOUT THE VOICE

Words in the script which appear in **bold-face** are the voice that the sisters hear in their dreams. Sometimes The Voice is narrating the sisters' dreams. Sometimes The Voice is prompting the sisters and sometimes it is The Voice that the sisters have heard in their dreams the night before.

In all these situations, The Voice should be the amplified or prerecorded version of the actor who plays Myra and Myrna. At times, the director may choose within a scene to have Myra or Myrna speak in tandem with The Voice.

The result should be a sound impossible to ignore or resist, just like the voice that used to come over the intercom in homeroom. Either brainwashing or subliminal seduction, this Voice is the way the sisters talk to each other. In Dreams.

With the single exception of Sarah, all the characters above should be played in a constant state of high hormonal excitement.

THE MINEOLA TWINS

ACT ONE

Dream Sequence Number One

Eerie lighting Myra Richards, age seventeen, stands in a trance, in a letter sweater with several M's stitched on askew; it looks like bloody hands have clutched and stretched the knit during an apocalyptic Sock Hop that ended in disaster. Spooky 1950's sci-fi movie music. The Voice comments to us:

Dream Sequence Number One. Myra In Homeroom. Myra In Hell.

A flash of lightning. A crackle of thunder.

MYRA. So. It was like homeroom, only we were calculating the hypotenuse of hygiene. I whispered to Billy Bonnell — what does that mean? And he said: Yuck-yuck — it's the same angle as the triangle under your skirt, Myra Richards. Yuck-yuck.

Shut-Up Creep! Thhwwack! My metal straight edge took off the top of his cranium. And then Mrs. Hopkins said, in this voice from the crypt: Miss Richards — what is the hypotenuse of hygiene?

And just as I was saying Excuse Me, Mrs. Hopkins, But I Didn't Know What the Homework Was for Today on Account of Being Suspended Last Week By You 'Cause of the Dumb-Ass Dress Code —

The Voice Cuts In on the Intercom:
"... Get ... To ... The ... Door ... Now."
And we all got real scared. And the Nuclear Air Raid Siren

Came On, Real Loud. And kids started bawling and scrambling under their desks. Somehow we knew it was For Real. We could hear this weird whistling of the bombs coming for us, with a straight line drawn from Moscow to Mineola. Dead Center for the Nassau County Court House. Dead Center for Roosevelt Field. And Dead Center for Mineola High. Home of the Mineola Mustangs.

And I knew it would do diddly-squat to get under the desk. Something drew me into the hall, where there was pulsing Red Light and Green Smoke.

Like Christmas in Hell.

I just kept walking.

Kids' bodies were mangled everywhere. In the middle of the hall, Our Principal Mr. Chotner was hypotenusing under Miss Dorothy Comby's skirt.

I just kept walking.

The girls' Glee Club had spread-eagled Mr. Koch the driver's ed instructor further down the hall, and they were getting the long-handled custodian's broom out of the closet.

I just kept walking.

I checked my watch. Five minutes to the Apocalypse. I could hear the bombs humming louder now. I thought of crossing against the lights and getting home. But there's nothing lonelier than watching your parents hug while you curl up on the rug alone and Mom's ceramic dogs melt on the mantle as the sky glows its final Big Red.

Then I heard **The Voice** on the intercom say to me:

"... **Find ... Her ...**"

I had to Obey The Voice.

I knew that at the bottom of the stairwell, I would find my twin sister Myrna, hiding from me. Curled up in a little O, her back to me. Just like Old Times in the Womb. *(The Voice begins to breathe rapidly into the microphone.)*

I entered the stairwell at the top. The lights were out. The air was thick. The stairs were steep. And I heard her soft breathing, trying not to breathe.

She could hear me breathe.

Her soft throat, trying not to swallow. *(The amplified sound of The Voice gulping.)*

She could taste my saliva.

Her heart, trying not to beat. *(The amplified sound of a beating heart.)*

She could hear my heart thunder. *(The heart beats faster.)*

She knew I was there.

And I said: **"I'm Coming, Myrna."**

"I'm Coming ... to Find ... You..." *(Teresa Brewer's "Sweet Old Fashioned Girl"* plays into the next scene.)*

---

*See Special Note on Songs and Recordings on copyright page.

Scene 1

1950's

Myrna Richards, age seventeen, is in the midst of closing up the local luncheonette, early evening. Jim Tracey, age twenty-two, in neat attire, prepares to smoke a pipe while waiting for Myrna. As the play begins, Myrna is waving good-bye to a customer who has left.

MYRNA. 'Night, Mr. Hawkins! Thanks for the tip! Yes, you're right, a dime certainly doesn't go as far as it did — *(Myrna spies Mr. Hawkins' cane, still perched on the counter by his stool.)* — Wait! Mr. Hawkins! Your cane! *(Myrna turns towards us and we see her high school clothes are protected by a demure apron. She quickly retrieves the cane, exits offstage, and returns to the doorway.)* — You're welcome! That's right! Now you can go home and 'thwack' Mrs. Hawkins with it! Ha-ha! Good night, now! *(Myrna closes the door to the luncheonette, and flips the "Closed" sign towards the street.)* Such a *nice* man. *(Myrna wipes the counter, straightens chairs. Jim succeeds in lighting his pipe. Myrna sniffs the air in alarm.)* Did I turn off the grill? I smell something burning — *(Myrna turns and sees Jim smoking his pipe.)* Oh, Goodness, Jim!
JIM. Do you like it? I got it today!
MYRNA. Golly! Now I'm engaged to a man who smokes a pipe!
JIM. Well, there we were in the office, puffing cigarettes in the marketing session, trying to come up with ideas for this new car that Ford is designing. And that's when it hit me. I thought: that's it! A pipe!
MYRNA. Very dashing.
JIM. *(Suddenly anxious.)* But I don't look … "intellectual," do I?
MYRNA. Oh no. Not at all.
JIM. I don't want to stand out too much.
MYRNA. Oh you don't. That's why I fell so hard for you — the way you just blend in.

JIM. Maybe this wasn't such a good idea. After all, Arthur Miller smokes a pipe ...

MYRNA. Isn't he the baseball player?

JIM. Darling. That's Joe DiMaggio.

MYRNA. Oh well, you know how I am with names in the newspaper ... Arthur Miller, Joe DiMaggio, Joseph Stalin — you're my window on the world. *(Jim puffs importantly.)*

JIM. So what's wrong, kitten? I thought we'd agreed not to see each other on school nights.

MYRNA. Oh I know. But I'm so upset, Jim, and I don't know where else to turn — *(Jim takes Myrna in his arms.)*

JIM. Tell Big Jim.

MYRNA. *(Breaking away.)* Oh it's that sister of mine again! I swear the Devil rocked her cradle when Mom was out of the room!

JIM. Oh now, Myra's a little wild, that's all.

MYRNA. — There's such meanness in her! I'd swear someone dumped her on our doorstep if it wasn't that we're identical twins —

JIM. — Almost identical. Besides, everyone fights with their siblings —

MYRNA. — I've tried. I really have. We decided, fair and square, to divide the room into equal halves ... I drew an imaginary line down the middle, and I said to Myra, reasonably, that she was not to cross that line. Except in the case of fire or nuclear emergencies.

JIM. That sounds sensible.

MYRNA. If she wants to live in squalor and chaos and *utter filth*, that's fine, that's fine, just do in on *her half*. Except. Except! She discards her dirty socks on my side of the room. How does she get those socks so *dirty*?

JIM. When we get married, you won't have to put up with her dirty socks anymore — you'll only have to put up with mine —

MYRNA. — No, Jim, it's gotten really, really bad. Mom and Daddy had a big blowup with Myra. She's been sneaking out of the house, late at night, to go downtown and God Knows Where Else with those boys she hangs out with — maybe even *Greenwich Village* —

JIM. Well, Greenwich Village isn't exactly Sodom and Gomorrah —

MYRNA. I don't know, Jim. There are an awful lot of girls wearing *pants* down there. *(Very slight shudder.)* Anyway, there's been a horrible, horrible fight. Daddy found out that ... that Myra's gotten a job in a road-side tavern of ill repute — as a so-called "cocktail waitress!"

JIM. What was your father doing in a house of ill repute?

MYRNA. He said he was having car trouble, and went into the Tic Tock to use the phone — and saw Myra in a skimpy outfit waiting on *men his own age!*

JIM. Well, I'm sure she'll make good wages in tips —

MYRNA. Jim! Mineola is a small but decent town! We can't let Myra ruin our good name!

JIM. Well, why doesn't your father go talk to her?

MYRNA. Oh, you know Daddy. He's a man who doesn't show his feelings. Or speak, for that matter. He's so sweet and tired when he comes home. He just sits in his rocking chair, thumping the arms of his chair. But I can tell he's upset. He's rocking much faster, and thumping and thumping away like his heart is breaking. He even talked at the dinner table last night. He called Myra a Whore of Babylon. But I know he doesn't mean it. He's never even *been* to Babylon.

JIM. Then why don't you have a heart-to-heart between two sisters?

MYRNA. I really wish we could be closer ... but she ... scares me.

JIM. She scares you!

MYRNA. No, really, Jim — there's something ... evil in her. I get scared when ... I look into her eyes. And then I have the most awful *nightmares.* I dream I'm in homeroom when the air raid siren comes on and even though it's the end of the civilized world as we know it, Myra tracks me down and ... and ... I can't remember. And then I wake up.

JIM. I see. I suppose you want me to talk to her.

MYRNA. Oh Jim, would you? **... Find Her.** She's got to quit that job. I know she'd listen to you. I don't think I can hold up my head in this town anymore. And I've been trying so hard for the Homemakers of America Senior Award.

JIM. Honey, people don't mistake you for your sister. You're two separate people.

MYRNA. It's gotten really bad. This past Sunday, I was conducting class for the Catholic Youth Organization, and I saw Davy Fowler passing a note to Billy Dicktel — so I confiscated it. And

read it. And were my cheeks red!
JIM. What did the note say?
MYRNA. It's hard for me to say. Don't look at me. It said … it said … "what does Myra Richards say … after … she … has sex?" *(Myrna blushes bright red.)*

JIM. *(Simultaneously.)*	MYRNA. *(Simultaneously.)*
"Are all you guys on the same same team?"	"Are all you guys on the same same team?"

(Jim starts to laugh, and stops.)
JIM. Sorry. Okay, princess. Let me see that pretty little smile of yours, and I'll drop in on the Tic Toc tonight, okay? *(Myrna comes into his arms and puts on her bravest smile.)* That's my girl!
MYRNA. But you won't "tarry" in the Tic Toc, will you Jim? Because if you do — "**I'm Coming To Find You.**" *(Jim stares a moment at Myrna; she lightens her tone.)* Because sometimes I worry — what if all the other girls find out about my special older man and try to steal him from me?
JIM. What if the football captain happens to glance your way?
MYRNA. The football captain? *(Myrna's face falls.)* I think … he's already scored a touchdown at my sister's goal-post.
JIM. Whoops … What about the captain of the wrestling team?
MYRNA. Myra was pinned on the mat in round one!
JIM. Track?
MYRNA. Myra's Three-minute Mile?!
JIM. Golf Team?
MYRNA. Myra's Hole-in —
JIM. — Okay. What if … the captain of the Chess Team looks your way?
MYRNA. *He's* out of luck. I know what I want. It's going to be so grand. In just another year, I'll be out of high school, and I've saved my pennies from waiting tables to take courses from Katherine Gibbs —
JIM. — Except I don't want my wife to work!
MYRNA. Oh I won't for long! Just long enough for us to save a down payment on a little two bedroom Levittown home.
JIM. If everything goes well with this new ad campaign for Ford — you won't have to work. The bonuses will be pouring in!
MYRNA. Oh. My. That sounds exciting. *(Myrna gets flushed.*

They start to make out.)
JIM. I'm pledged to secrecy — but you've never seen anything like this car! When it hits, it's going to hit big! The firm's even hiring this poetess to come up with lyrical names — like Fiesta or Bronco or Ford Epiphany! — And wait 'til you see the grille on this baby — well, I helped a little to come up with the design — it looks just like — like — *(Jim gets flushed.)* — Well, I can't say. Guys are gonna go crazy over this buggy! Honey, the future is ours! You can stay home and cook to your heart's content! You won't have to go to Katherine Gibbs!
MYRNA. Well, a girl should always be prepared for the future. Once I've learned stenography and typing — when my rising young executive-husband comes home with work from the office — he can put his feet up on the hassock while I Take Dictation. We'll have a son, and by the time he's three or four, we can afford a three-bedroom house in Great Neck with an office downstairs. Then we'll have a dog, and maybe a daughter, too.
JIM. — Kitten. Maybe we should let some things be a surprise — *(Appropriate music, like Doris Day's "I'll See You In My Dreams"* starts to play from the jukebox.)*
MYRNA. Oh, I know what kind of surprises you want. Just like a man. You've been spending time reading Mr. Hefner again, haven't you?
JIM. I'm a lonely man on school nights.
MYRNA. Oh Jim. I know. I miss you too on school nights. *(They begin to make out seriously now.)* I … I just … count … the minutes until … Friday night.
JIM. MMmmm. Me Too. I can't keep my mind on work. *(Jim shifts Myrna's weight against him.)*
MYRNA. You … you don't mind, do you, Jim? Waiting for me?
JIM. It's … hard. Awfully … hard. Myrna — *(Jim has started to loosen Myrna's items of clothing.)*
MYRNA. Oh … Jim. Jim … *(Myrna starts to help him.)* — Wait — I'm getting choked a little — there. That's better.
JIM. You've put the "Closed" sign up, didn't you?
MYRNA. We're locked up … "tight."
JIM. Quick … turn off the overhead lights — *(Myrna complies.*

---

*See Special Note on Songs and Recordings on copyright page.

She comes back, panting slightly.)
MYRNA. My. This *is* a treat for a school night. *(Jim lifts Myrna up on a stool. She wraps herself around him. Suddenly, Myrna stops, puzzled.)* Jim. How come, if Myra and I are identical twins, that we're not ... identical? I mean, how come she's ...
JIM. Flat as a pancake?
MYRNA. *(Giggling.)* True. And I'm so ...
JIM. Stacked, darling. Like a stack of pancakes.
MYRNA. Yes. But I mean, is it scientifically possible? Wouldn't either both of us be ... you know — *(Myrna runs her hands coquettishly over her breasts.)* —
JIM. Yes, yes — *(Jim starts unsnapping Myrna's brassiere beneath her blouse.)*
MYRNA. — Or we'd both be like Iowa in the chestal region? *(Jim now helps Myrna step out of her underwear beneath her skirt.)*
JIM. You're just lucky, I guess. I'm ... just lucky. Please, God, let me be lucky tonight — *(Jim nibbles on Myrna's neck. She moans.)*
MYRNA. Bloodlines ... science and *all that* ... it's just ... so ... strange.
JIM. Let's not talk about your sister anymore tonight. Let's not talk. *(Jim presses against Myrna; throughout the following the petting gets hotter until Myrna clambers up on all fours onto two adjoining stools and Jim gets on his knees on the adjacent stool.)*
MYRNA. Oh! Oh Jim! Oh ... Oh Jim!
JIM. Myrna ...
MYRNA. Jim, Jim, Jim —
JIM. *(Urgently.)* Myrna, Myrna —
MYRNA. Yes! Right now! Jim! Now! Now! Ohhh — Jimboooohhh — WAIT! *(Jim red-faced and behind Myrna, stops stock-still.)* Jim — this — this isn't right.
JIM. Oh, Myrna —
MYRNA. These stools are giving me motion sickness. *(Myrna climbs down with iron will.)* We ... we shouldn't be doing this. *(Myrna looks behind and sees Jim rotating on his stool in frustration. She stops him from spinning.)* Darling — I want you. Badly. But not now. Not here. I want it to be so ... right. Not with the smell of meatloaf still in the air. And it will ... it will be ... so "right," won't it? Jim?

JIM. I guess. *(Jim and Myrna do not speak to each other for a beat. They adjust their clothing. Myrna picks up her undies with great dignity, tucking the cotton into her apron pockets.)*
MYRNA. I want to be pure for you on our Wedding Day.
JIM. Oh, Myrna … You are pure. You have been pure. You will always be pure.
MYRNA. No, Jim — I have to earn the right to wear white when I walk down the aisle. It's different for men. There are no absolutes for guys.
JIM. But, Myrna, Baby —
MYRNA. No Buts. It's the Domino Theory. First I say good-bye to my virginity — then I start smoking outside the house, piercing my ears, wearing ruby red lipstick, chewing gum and buying TV dinners! Then where would we all be. *(Jim sighs wearily.)* Oh my. I haven't filled the sugar and condiment bottles yet. *(There is an awkward pause as Jim finds his pipe and knocks out the ashes.)* Please, darling. Tell me you understand. *(Jim's Adam's apple bobs as he speaks.)*
JIM. I understand, Myrna. You're a good girl. It's just that God built Men with this … "design flaw." It's not great for an automotive body much less the engine to torque it up like that without letting the throttle go. *(Myrna, concerned, turns to Jim to touch him.)*
MYRNA. Oh Jim. I'm so sorry.
JIM. Don't *touch* me. Not right now. I've got to. … let the engine cool down.
MYRNA. Oh Jim. I don't understand about these things. But if there was … something … something I could do without compromising my innocence … something that … might make you feel better — would you tell me? *(Jim thinks a moment, tempted. Then his better angel decides.)*
JIM. Maybe I'd better go. It's getting late. *(Jim takes a huge breath.)* There. It's not … "hurting" as much now. I think I can walk.
MYRNA. Jim!
JIM. You are so … good. You're the only absolute goodness in my life. Let's say good night while we have no regrets.
MYRNA. You're my guiding light, Jim. Will I see you Friday night? *(Jim half-hobbles, half-sidles in a strange crab-walk to the luncheonette door.)*

JIM. You bet. *(He manages a half-smile from the doorway.)* I'd better find that sister of yours and give her a talking to.
MYRNA. Good night, Jim!
JIM. Good night, Darling. *(Jim exits. Myrna flies to the door, and waves angelically at his retreating figure.)*
MYRNA. 'Til Friday! *(Myrna turns, worry now on her face. In a whisper, she addresses the Deity in the hush of the luncheonette:)* Please, God, Please — let Jim wait for me! *(Fifties music swells as the lights dim into Scene 2.)*

Scene 2

Later that evening. We see the interior of a cheap motel used for trysts of G.I.'s on leave from Mitchel Air Force Base. The blinking neon of "MOTEL" flashes throughout the scene. At the start of scene, Myra sits up in bed, agitated. She wears a push-up Maidenform and a panty-girdle. Myra manages to smoke furiously while cracking her gum. There is a heap in the bed beside her, curled under the cheap chintz spread, completely covered, and hogging the entire bedspread. Occasionally, we hear muffled sobs.

MYRA. *(Myra nudges the heap.)* Hey. Hey. You gonna come out sometime this decade? *(The heap covers itself with some insistence.)* Hey. Suit yourself, daddy-O. No skin offa my pearlie-whites. I've had cats cry before the Act, and I've had lottsa cats wail during. You're the first one to boo-hoo after. *(Myra tries again.)* Hey, I gotta idea. You got any bread? You got wheels. We could just spook in your bomb and spin into the Village. It's crazy down there, any night of the week. We go take in the Vanguard — do you dig that scene? It's the most, the meanest … we could do a set, then blow the joint and just walk around the streets. There's this one guy, Ace, who walks around with a *parrot* on his shoulder. It's crazy. He's so hip — you pay him a dime, and he gives you a poem

on the spot. He poetizes on a dime. And these poems — they don't rhyme or anything. They're deep. They don't *mean*, they just *are*. It's far-out! *(Jim, in a fury, pops up.)*
JIM. Speak English, can't you! If you want to talk to me, speak English! English!
MYRA. Wow. *(Jim huddles, still clutching the spread around him.)*
JIM. Jesus. You've watched too many James Dean movies. *(Myra chokes up at the mention of James Dean.)*
MYRA. He only made *three*. And then he *died*.
JIM. Hey, look, I wasn't making fun of him or anything.
MYRA. He was important to a lot of people. He lived fast, died young ... and really messed up his face.
JIM. I'm sure he was important to impressionable young women. But that doesn't mean he could act. Couldn't drive, either.
MYRA. Oh, he could drive. It was the yo-yo on the other side of the yellow line he didn't count on. I'll bet he was going over a hundred in that Spyder, the top down, he was flying, he was putting something down! Some ass-hole yo-yo in a *Ford*, for God's sake. *(Jim clears his throat.)*
JIM. The Ford Motor Company happens to be one of my clients.
MYRA. Oh. What do you do for them?
JIM. Well, I advise them on strategies for younger buyers under twenty-five. We're devising a new model that's going to sweep aside the competition.
MYRA. So where is this company of yours where you work at devising and sweeping?
JIM. Madison Avenue.
MYRA. You work in Manhattan? And you don't live there?
JIM. I like more air and more space and more *green*.
MYRA. Oh man. You're free, white, over twenty-one, and you get to get up every morning and take the LI — double — R into Manhattan. If I were you, I'd cash in the return ticket to Mineola and find a pad like — *(Snap.)* — that.
JIM. You'll get your chance.
MYRA. Not soon enough.
JIM. There's nothing wrong with Mineola.
MYRA. *(Exploding.)* What is there to do in Mineola? Go to bingo, go to the PTA, fight over whether or not *Catcher in the Rye*

should be allowed in our libraries! Mineola's so dull, there wasn't even a Red Scare here! In Mineola, people keep their blinds up because *nothing happens* on a Saturday night.
JIM. You are full of hate.
MYRA. I'm restless! Don't you sometimes feel like you're gonna jump out of your skin if you don't do something, go somewhere?
JIM. Well, sometimes.
MYRA. Yeah? And then what do you do?
JIM. I go for a nice, brisk walk around the block. *(Myra heads for her leather coat and the door.)*
MYRA. Catch you later.
JIM. Wait, wait! — this fellow with the parrot — Ace?
MYRA. Yeah, Ace.
JIM. What is his poetry like?
MYRA. It's hard to describe in words. It's like jazz riffs without the music. It's just a torrent of feeling and colors and *truth*.
JIM. No rhyme?
MYRA. Rhyme is out. Square. Dead.
JIM. Look, I've read *On the Road*.
MYRA. You have?
JIM. Yes. In hard-cover. *(Myra is impressed.)*
MYRA. You're okay for a man who wears ties.
JIM. You're okay, too. You're nothing like your sister — *(It strikes Jim.)* — Oh my God! Your sister! Oh, God, Oh God —
MYRA. Look don't clutch on me, Jim ... Hang Loose, okay? Just breathe. It's gonna be all right.
JIM. Oh, man, what am I going to tell her?
MYRA. She doesn't ask, you don't tell. Don't ask, Don't tell. The formula for modern marriage.
JIM. Oh, God. She'll look into my eyes. She'll know.
MYRA. What, you think your eyes are gonna look different now? Oh, boy, where did you get your information? Health classes at Mineola High?
JIM. I've got to think. You've got to help me think.
MYRA. Although I bet you are going to walk in a different way. You know what they call it when they lower the front end of a car to stream-line it? So it's real fast for dragging? They call it "raking." And that's you, daddy-o. You've been raked.

JIM. I've got to think. *(Myra snaps her gum.)* Could you maybe not pop your gum? *(Myra, with great ceremony, removes her gum and places it on the headboard.)*
MYRA. Okay, now we can think great thoughts.
JIM. Wait until you get married!
MYRA. Hardehar-har. There's never been a movie made that's even close to how I'm gonna live. I'm making it up from scratch. No marriage. No children. No suburbs. Just freedom!
JIM. But you're a girl! You can't do that!
MYRA. I am going to spend my life doing everything people tell me I can't do. *(Beat.)*
JIM. Maybe I should think over this marriage thing.
MYRA. Look, Jim — you gotta marry my sister. She's been collecting recipes until she has dinner completely planned for the first year.
JIM. Are you hot? There's no air in here —
MYRA. Oh shit. She's gonna blame me.
JIM. No. It's the domino theory. There goes my virginity, my work ethic, monogamy, raising 2.5 children, truth in advertising, living in the suburbs, caring for my aged parents and saluting the flag. I've been raked.
MYRA. Wow. Heavy. *(Jim and Myra sit next to each other in bed. Contemplate.)* My brain hurts. That usually never happens *after* sex.
JIM. Yeah. I guess.
MYRA. So this was your first time..
JIM. Yes ... Myra? Was I — could you tell me — was I —
MYRA. You were wonderful, Jimmy. You know, I've never known any one like you, Jim Tracy. You're the kind of guy a girl could dream about.
JIM. Thanks ... Myra? How "many" guys have you —
MYRA. Gone all the way with? To Home Plate?
JIM. Yes. Do you mind my asking?
MYRA. Well, there are all the guys on the first string — and I'm working on the second string who have their letters —
JIM. Whoa! So it's really true about you. You really are the Whore of Babylon!
MYRA. Hey! Wait a minute! First of all, I happen to really like football. Second of all, you just went all the way to home plate, same as I did. So where do you get off calling me that? Putting that down?

JIM. It's different for you — you're a girl. There are ... absolutes in the world for girls. Girls don't do, they just are. *(Furious, Myra gets out of bed and starts dressing. She tries not to cry.)*
MYRA. Why — why did you have to do this? I thought ... for a minute — I thought you were different. I thought you understood.
JIM. Why are you getting all steamed up? I'm just another 'notch' on your belt, right?
MYRA. — I hope my next decade is better than this one.
JIM. I mean, girls are born the way they are. Men *become*.
MYRA. I can't believe I fall for it every time.
JIM. Myrna was born "good." You were born ... "nice."
MYRA. I'm cool to the guys, thinking, dip that I am, that they're gonna be cool back. I don't get it, I really don't. I'm nice to you, right? I made you feel good, I felt good, we both felt good together, no questions asked, no demands — why then do you guys always do this?
JIM. So the bottom line is — you did sleep with the football team. *(Myra reaches the door, disheveled but dressed. She turns, goes back for her gum on the headboard.)*
MYRA. Well, lucky for us one of us had some experience. *(Myra puts the gum in her mouth. Just then, there is a timid tapping on the motel room door. Myra and Jim freeze.)*
MYRNA. *(Offstage — sobbing.)* Jim? Jim? ... Jiiimm?
MYRA. *(Hissed.)* Shit!
JIM. *(Feverishly whispered.)* O migod ... o migod ... omigod —
MYRA. Is this like the goddamn Alamo? Or is there a backdoor? *(Jim puts his trousers on backwards; Myra checks out the bathroom.)*
MYRNA. *(Off.)* Oh, Jim — I know you're in there. I know, Jim. You're in there with — *(Sob.)* HER. *(There is a continued sobbing and tapping on the door.)*
MYRA. *(Stage whisper.)* There's a window over the toilet — it's gonna be a tight squeeze — lucky for me I don't have any tits. Give me the keys to your car. *(Sob/Tap on the door. Jim is in a state of shock. Myra grabs him.)* Your car. Your car, daddy-o. Give Me the Goddamn Keys. Now. *(Jim reaches into his trouser pockets awkwardly; she grabs the keys out of his shaking hands.)* Kiss Her Good Night for me. I'm outta here. *(Myra rushes into the bathroom. We hear a window being pried open, a faint "oooff" of pain, and a*

thud. Meanwhile on the front door, the wounded thrush tapping has changed into the staccato pounding of a killer.)
MYRNA. *(Off.)* MYRA! I'M GONNA KILL YOU, MYRA! WAIT 'TIL I GET MY HANDS AROUND YOUR SCRAWNY LITTLE NECK! MYRA! YOU SUCK, MYRA! I'M GONNA RIP OFF WHAT LITTLE THERE IS OF YOUR KNOCKERS, MYRA! I'M GONNA USE YOUR ITSIES FOR MY KEY-CHAIN, MYRA! I WILL NEVER TALK TO YOU AGAIN! OPEN— *(Pound.)* THIS *(Pound.)* DOOR! *(Pound.) (A huge thump. A beat. Then, the wounded thrush tactic again. The sound of a tremulous little girl writhing against the door in agony, who wouldn't hurt a fly, but might slash her wrists. Little butterfly sobs of pathos; off.)* J-jiimm? Baby? Jjiimm-bo? Honey — I know it isn't your fault. I know how good you are ... baby — just let me in, let me see you, Jim ... don't send me away ... Jimm? Jimmy? Jimmy-Jim? *(Jim, moved, scared, catatonic, sidles to the door with his backwards trousers falling down. He tentatively unlocks the door.)*
JIM. *(Sobbing.)* Myrna? Baby? There's — there's no one here — *(As Myrna hears the door lock click, she throws herself into the room with a Medea-scream:)*
MYRNA. I'LL KILL YOU!!! *(Jim lands on his butt. Myrna flies across the room. They blink at each other in the disheveled room. As Myrna picks up something from the floor, there is the sound of Jim's automobile being quickly started, revved, and thrown into reverse outside the room:)* Shhh — ootttt! *(Myrna runs to the door, too late. She watches a car offstage screech out of the parking lot into the night. Her shoulders slump. Jim huddles where he is. A beat. Myrna turns, limp and tired, with a single dirty sock that Myra has cast off dangling from her hand in silent accusation. They both stare at the sock.)*

BLACKOUT

Scene 3

1969

We see Myrna, muffled in a trench coat, a head scarf and dark glasses, standing in line for a teller at the Roosevelt Savings and Loan in downtown Mineola. She is visibly paranoid, checking around her while trying to remain discrete. Myrna has hardened slightly, small lines of discontent forming around her mouth. She is a woman who continues to embrace the fifties; only the hem of her skirt tells us it is actually 1969.

Beside her is her son Kenny, a slight, sensitive teenager, dressed in a paisley shirt and blue bell-bottom denims with a button fly. Kenny is listening to a brand new transistor radio.

KENNY. They're still hunting! She's the last one of the gang still on the loose! That guy who was the leader was killed in a shoot-out up-state! Whoa! But there's no sign of her!
MYRNA. If you're not going to listen to Casey Casem, young man, you are to turn your radio off. *Now. (A beat. They move up in the line.)* What happened to that poor guard?
KENNY. Still in the hospital.
MYRNA. I can't believe a member of my immediate family attacked someone in uniform. They are going to nail her hiney.
KENNY. Only if they catch her.
MYRNA. If there's any justice in this world, Aunt Myra will be making license plates the rest of her life. That should help put an end to the War in Vietnam. Instead of shacking up with radicals and the SDS, she'll have to fend off hefty female inmates in the shower when she drops her soap!
KENNY. Mom!
MYRNA. Well, for heaven's sake, Kenny, I know she's family, but

she should use common sense! How does — *(Myrna lowers her voice.)* — how does holding up the Roosevelt Savings and Loan in downtown Mineola help in ending the War!

KENNY. All I know is this is the most exciting thing to happen on Long Island Ever! *(Beat. They wait in the bank line.)*

MYRNA. What really gripes my A-S-S is I'm now a prisoner in my own house! I moved us to a nice neighborhood in Great Neck; I volunteered for the Nixon for President Campaign. I leafleted downtown for harsh control of subversives. And now gentlemen who look like Mormon Missionaries are parked outside my door in unmarked white Fords drinking coffee in Styrofoam cups! *(The two move up in line.)* When your Aunt Myra held up this bank, knowing darn well your grandmother and my joint savings is in here, she deliberately padded her brassiere so she could pass as me! My sister used my knockers as terrorist camouflage!

KENNY. Mom! *(Just then, two men who look like Mormon Missionaries in trench coats holding Styrofoam cups enter and stand casually by a counter.)* I think they're here.

MYRNA. My taxes are paying for this. *(Beat.)* It would have been nice, son, if you hadn't changed out of your nice school clothes that I just bought for you. *(Pause. Myrna and Kenny move up in line.)*

KENNY. It's bad enough that I have to dress like a Hitler Youth all day in school because of our Nazi principal and his Nazi dress code.

MYRNA. Kenny! Lower your voice. No one wants to hear your counter-cultural nonsense.

KENNY. It's the *Truth*.

MYRNA. You Make Me Laugh. If it wasn't for your grandfather and other men like him who fought for your freedom, you'd be singing "Deutsch Land Uber Alles" every morning in homeroom. — Nazis! Hitler Youth!

KENNY. Yeah! What about Mayor Daley's stormtroopers at the Democratic Convention?

MYRNA. — I do not want to have this discussion with you in public. It is not a good time right now. You could have a little concern for your mother's nerves right now and do your utmost to not attract attention. I wish I could be a teenager again. Everything's an absolute: Good, Evil; Black, White; Muskie, Nixon. There's no gray. Nothing relative. Just you passing judgment. It must be

wonderful to be fourteen and perfect, absolutely in the right, absolutely — *(Myrna suddenly stops and has a strange comatose seizure; we hear the echo of electric shock therapy. Kenny also stops, and watches her in alarm and guilt.)*
KENNY. *(Whispered.)* Mom? *(Kenny waits, we hear the electric buzzing start to fade)* Mom? Mom! *(Kenny shakes her. Myrna "comes to.")* You went off again.
MYRNA. Sorry. *(Beat.)*
KENNY. What happens to you? When you … go off … like that?
MYRNA. It's nothing to be scared about, Kenny. It's just a residual effect of the … the therapy I had.
KENNY. But what's it like? Where do you go?
MYRNA. I go back to a more peaceful time. Back to high school. When I still had a shot at the Homemaker's of America Senior Award. Long before I *was* a homemaker.
KENNY. Do you want to go home?
MYRNA. I'm fine.
KENNY. Is Dad coming home tonight? *(Myrna's mouth tightens slightly.)*
MYRNA. No. It will be just the two of us — having a wonderful time: a private date with a very handsome young beau — a few candles, and a new recipe. A special casserole with pineapple fritters!
KENNY. Yes ma'am … Can we have hamburger sometime this week?
MYRNA. You don't like my casseroles.
KENNY. They're … different.
MYRNA. Ever since my "medication" and "treatment" — something's happened to all my casseroles. Before I went into the hospital, I was a wonderful cook.
KENNY. You're still an okay cook, Mom.
MYRNA. Well. By-gone days. *(Jim Tracy, now down on his luck, in shoddy clerical attire, stands in the cashier's cage. Myrna and Kenny are now first in line.)*
JIM. Next.
MYRNA. Oh, Lord. Is there another cashier available?
KENNY. Go on, Mom. That man has called you.
MYRNA. Kenny — go to the counter over there and wait for me. *(Kenny complies. He looks at the FBI agents who sip their coffee and look at him. Myrna advances to the cashier cage. Jim tries to be offi-*

cious, but the exchange breaks into urgent whispering.)
JIM. How may I help you?
MYRNA. I'd like to make a withdrawal from a joint savings account — here. I expect you'll want to verify the signature.
JIM. That's fine ... Myrna!
MYRNA. *(Stiffly.)* Please. It's Mrs. O'Brien.
JIM. But you're well?
MYRNA. I'm fine, thank you. I'd appreciate large bills, please.
JIM. Yes, Mrs. O'Brien — May I tell you how sorry I am about the trouble with your sister?
MYRNA. I think that's in questionable taste.
JIM. Oh for God's sake, Myrna! Can't you just talk to me a little?
MYRNA. Would you please expedite my withdrawal? My son is with me, and I'm in a bit of a hurry —
JIM. Just look at me, just a little, Myrna — *(Myrna looks at him. Beat.)*
MYRNA. When's the last time you bought a proper suit? And a nice tie?
JIM. I know. I — I have ... nothing.
MYRNA. Is this what you want for yourself? To be a ... "bank cashier?"
JIM. At least I get to see you once a week. I tried bagging groceries at your A&P, but I wasn't fast enough.
MYRNA. What is it you want from me?
JIM. Couldn't we just have lunch together? Myrna? At our old luncheonette? Just ... lunch?
MYRNA. I am a *married* woman.
JIM. I know but — do you love your husband?
MYRNA. *(A bit loudly.)* Do I have to call the manager? *(The agents look at them. Myrna and Jim recover their composure, and go back to surreptitious whispering.)*
JIM. That will not be necessary. Large bills, I believe you said?
MYRNA. Yes — that's right. *(Jim counts the money, biting his lip.)* Thank you. *(As she starts to leave.)* For God's sake, Jim, go back to school, do something with your life, leave Mineola —! *(Jim brightens; Myrna has talked to him. She abruptly leaves.)*
JIM. Myrna! *(Myrna joins Kenny at the counter. The agents relax, study the income tax brochures and bank promotional literature.)*

MYRNA. I hate coming to this bank.
KENNY. Can we go now?
MYRNA. You know the story of the Prodigal Son? This man had two sons, right, and one worked hard in the fields from dawn to dusk. He never gave his parents cause to worry. The other son was a real *fuck-up*. I'm sorry, no other word will do. He never saved one thin dime, and he drank whatever money he filched from the family business. The Prodigal Son got into trouble with the law. He had to hide in this foreign land far across the borders, and a price was on his head. And he thought — Wait a minute, I'll bet I can get Mom sorry for me, and she'll dip into the old man's pockets when he's asleep. And so he came dragging home in clothes that hadn't been washed in weeks. And his aged parents bailed him out. They drew his bath water. They washed his clothes. And they barbecued up filet mignon. And do you know what the Good Son felt, when he came home from the fields and saw his evil brother getting the ticker-tape parade? *What am I, ground chuck? (Myrna stops. The buzzing is loud. Kenny waits, and then shakes her slightly.)*
KENNY. Mom? Mom? *(Myrna "comes to" and continues; the buzzing goes out.)*
MYRNA. The Good Brother bided his time, and then went to the cops in the other country and turned his sorry brother in. Took the reward, and invested it. And then, he got control of his father's business. He sent his parents to a nice, clean nursing home where they had arts therapy. And when the Prodigal Son was finally released from the hoosegow, he had to beg in the marketplace, until the Prodigal Son finally *died.* And the Good Son danced and danced. Happy Ending!
KENNY. I don't remember the story like that.
MYRNA. No? *(Myrna takes a breath.)* Now I want you to listen carefully to me, son. What your Aunt Myra did was wrong. This is our country, love it or leave it. *(Myrna takes another breath.)* But family is family. Blood is blood … *(Myrna and Kenny turn in the direction of the other counter where the agents are engrossed in their pamphlets and balancing their checkbooks. They turn back.)*
KENNY. Are we going to help Aunt Myra?
MYRNA. Yes. We are. You are. I'm asking you to be a grown man tonight, son. I can't go myself to help Myra — she only trusts you.

I am driving you to Bobby's house. I will drive off as a diversion, and the white unmarked Ford will follow me. When you are sure the coast is clear, slip out of Bobby's house by the back door, and walk to the train station. Get the 4:55 to New York. Aunt Myra says you're to get in the last car, and at each station change cars. That way you'll know if you're being followed. When you reach Penn Station, take the local IRT downtown to Astor Place. Walk carefully to St. Mark's Place, and then turn right on Second Avenue. Walk two blocks east on East Fifth St., and check if you're being followed. Go into the luncheonette on Fifth and First Avenue, and buy a hamburger and a Coke. Eat it slowly. Then retrace your steps to this address — *(Myrna hands Kenny a folded slip of paper.)* Aunt Myra is on the top floor, door to the left.
KENNY. Wow. Cool.
MYRNA. Above all else, do not walk around in the Village.
KENNY. What's wrong with the Village? The Village is safe!
MYRNA. Kenny. I'll be worried sick about you.
KENNY. Yes ma'am ... This is the most exciting day of my entire life. *(With solemnity, Myrna draws out a bulging envelope from her coat pocket.)*
MYRNA. I'm trusting you with a great deal, Kenny. The money inside the envelope is from Grandma. Grandma cashed in a $5,000 treasury bond for Myra.
KENNY. Whoa.
MYRNA. To help a criminal. That $5,000 should get Myra across the border into Canada. When Myra gets to Canada, she's to change her name, change her hair color, and copy *someone else's* face.
KENNY. Mom — What if Dad gets home before I do?
MYRNA. Okay, Kenny, it's cut the crap time. You and I both know your father's shacked up at the Plaza with his secretary for the rest of the weekend.
KENNY. She's nice. She likes to wear mauve. *(Myrna narrows her eyes with suspicion.)*
MYRNA. I don't like hearing the word "mauve" in your mouth. Only boys who grow up to be interior decorators use words like "mauve."
KENNY. Mom!
MYRNA. Maybe it's all that time Myra spent baby-sitting you

while I was "indisposed." In the "hospital." Myra was spoon-feeding you mashed banana and Mao Tse-Tung! And teaching you words like "Mauve!" *(The buzzing begins again; Kenny pleads.)*
KENNY. Please don't get upset. *(Myrna draws out something white from her coat pocket.)*
MYRNA. One last thing — you are to hand your Aunt Myra this. *(Beat.)*
KENNY. Why would I give her a dirty sock?
MYRNA. She'll know why. Say that the sock is from me. I've saved it all these many years just for a moment like this. Because many years ago, your Aunt Myra took something precious, someone very dear, and tossed it all away like a used sock. I want her to transport this dirty sock over the Canadian border. I want her to take her disrespect and her dirty sock with her. And when she misses all the wonderful things America has, she can finger this dirty sock and think about the choices she made. *(Beat.)* Meet me out front. I'll go get the car. *(As Myrna exits, the FBI agents hold open the door for her:)* Thank you, gentlemen. How's your coffee? *(Kenny, left behind for a second with Myra's sock in his hand, regards it with devotion. He feels someone staring at him; turns and sees Jim Tracy at the cashier's window. Kenny stuffs the sock in his pocket and runs after his mother. End of scene. Intermission.)*

ACT TWO

Dream Sequence Number Two

We see Myrna in a hospital johnny. Her hair has not been tended to in some time. Occasionally, there is an electronic buzzing underneath the institutional Muzak which begins to play. Two psychiatric aides run in slow motion behind Myrna; they catch up and restrain her, one at each elbow. The effect, though, is of a choreographed dance routine, which, in fact it is. Throughout the following monologue, Myrna spins beyond their reach; caught and lifted by each aide in turn, dipping and twirling. The aides are unable to fasten Myrna into a straitjacket. The Voice tells us:

Dream Sequence Number Two. Myrna in the Hospital. Myrna In Hell.

MYRNA. So. I will be dressed in my London Fog raincoat, with my Coach bag accessories, neatly coifed, because Dr. Prior says hygiene is a sign of mental health.

I'll park behind the trailer, next to the dump right off Jericho Turnpike. Then I'll knock at her screen door.

My sister will answer the door, still drowsy from her night shift. But she'll pretend not to be surprised.

"Can I come in?" I'll ask.

She turns and leaves the screen door open.

I enter. It's a pigsty; high-heels are dropped willy-nilly; dirty dishes pile in the sink. A trail of socks leads to the platform bed in the back.

She sits down at the table and waits.

"Listen — " I say: "can we have a cup of tea together?"
As she makes the tea, I chatter. She searches for a clean cup. It's not very. She pours the water. She dumps the cups on the table and the water sloshes over the rim of my cup. You'd swear she was never a

waitress. — "Oh — Myra," I say " — you've left the stove on!"

As my sister turns, swiftly I take the vial from my pocket and pour it into her cup. Then I quickly add two sugars and stir as she turns back —

"You do take sugar, don't you?" She does. I don't. I never have.

We sip our tea.

"There's bad blood between us. No one could clear up the bad blood.

Myra nods. Her head continues to nod in slower and slower circles. I catch the teacup before it falls, the drug already coursing through her blood.

Quickly I go to work. I put on my Playtex living gloves, my rain bonnet and my London Fog. I carefully wash her cup, and put it away. I put the suicide note on the table with the handwriting that looks just like hers, the letters trailing off after:

"I Can't Go On This Way…"

Then I open the trunk of my car and take out Daddy's hunting rifle. I giggle, because I'd never held anything more dangerous than a soup ladle.

But I know just what to do. Kneeling beside my sister, I take off her right shoe. I toss it on the floor. I take off her right sock — I just toss it. Then I brace the rifle at a jaunty angle so that her big toe jams the trigger while her mouth sucks the double barrel — just like old times with the football team. *(Amplified sound of breathing.)*

Then I kneel beside her and whisper: **"This is real, you asshole, this is happening."** *(Amplified sound of The Voice gulping.)*

For the first time in years, my sister and I touch as I press her big toe on the trigger. *(Amplified sound of a beating heart.)*

We squeeze the trigger together.

It sounds like *champagne*. I don't want to look. I expect to see hamburger, ground chuck at 49 cents a pound. But from the stem of her neck, where her head used to be — there's a bouquet. Her brains have flowered. *Les Fleurs du mal.* "It's so pretty, Myra!" I tell her. I touch a single stem. I'll take a flower home and press it in my diary.

Maybe when he's old enough, I'll give it to Kenny.

Kenny.

What am I going to tell little Kenny? *(The two psychiatric aides finally restrain Myrna in the jacket, but the three continue to dance the choreographed routine, in complete Hollywood harmony.)*

The truth. Tell Kenny the truth. *(Myrna smiles beatifically at her dance partners/keepers.)*

Aunt Myra has gone on a long, long trip. Far across the border. *(The smile turns into a grin.)*

And she's never coming back. *(The electronic buzzing grows as the aides escort Myrna offstage.)*

Scene 1

Later that evening. Myra sits on a mattress on a floor in an apartment in the East Village. There are political posters on the wall advertising marches, Jimi Hendrix, love, peace, etc. In one corner of the room, there is a bong; in another a lava lamp. There is a single chair. Myra sits cross-legged on the mattress, a roll of toilet paper beside her for Kleenex as she weeps. She clutches the dirty sock. Beside her is a can of Coca Cola. Kenny is lying on the floor on his stomach, his hand holding her.

MYRA. Kenny. Oh man, Kenny. Shit, Ken. *(Myra weeps into the sock. Kenny takes the sock away and hands Myra the toilet roll.)*
KENNY. Use the toilet paper, okay? You don't know where that sock has been.
MYRA. I really really really fucked up.
KENNY. It could be worse.
MYRA. Did they catch Hacker yet?
KENNY. Yeah. He might be dead or something.
MYRA. Oh man. First Malcolm, then Che and now — Hacker. Hacker. He was a maniac. He was kinda an asshole, too. But he was a great lover. Out of all the guys on the National Council, he was the best. *(She sniffles.)* Gave me chlamydia, too. That's what happens when you sleep with the leadership. Well, at least I'll have a keepsake.
KENNY. What's chlamydia?
MYRA. Oh, shit. You can't stay here. We've got to move.
KENNY. Nobody followed me.
MYRA. You sure?
KENNY. I was real careful.
MYRA. You're my brave, smart, nephew. How you can be my sister's son is one of those mysteries of genetics.
KENNY. Mom's pretty pissed.

MYRA. It's Grandma's money.
KENNY. I know.
MYRA. I'm gonna pay it back. I'm gonna get a good job in Toronto; no more collectives.
KENNY. I know.
MYRA. I've got to be on my guard. I've got to stay alert. *(Shakily, Myra draws out a pill.)*
KENNY. What's that?
MYRA. It's … "medicine." Methedrine. It keeps me awake. Can you hand me that Coke? *(Kenny hands Myra the Coke so she can down her pill.)*
KENNY. I thought you told me not to drink Coke. That the Coca-Cola company was a mega-conglamorate whose imperialist profits fuel the war.
MYRA. *(Enjoying the Coke.)* Ah … It's true. But it's got caffeine. Sometimes you've got to use the system to crush the system.
KENNY. That is so true.
MYRA. What happened to the guard I hit?
KENNY. She's okay. She's gonna lose her little toe on her left foot. The one you ran over. Mom say's they're gonna nail you for attacking someone in uniform.
MYRA. I didn't see her in my rear view mirror. There she was, with her bright orange safety patrol sling, signaling traffic, and the next thing I know, she's screaming and holding her foot and hopping to the curb.
KENNY. It was an accident. You didn't mean to run over her little toe. It's gonna be okay.
MYRA. I'm really strung-out. I can't move like this. I'm going to take one toke for the road, just to take the edge off. *(Myra lights a joint; Kenny perks up expectantly as Myra starts to toke up. Myra inhales several puffs expertly.)* Cannabis always calms me down. Want some? *(Kenny is thrilled, takes the joint. Inhales. Myra starts to giggle. Kenny starts giggling too.)*
KENNY. What's so funny?
MYRA. *(Holding the sock.)* She kept it in Tupperware? *(Kenny nods, still smoking, laughing.)* In the back of the freezer? *(They splutter with laughter.)* She's gotta get out of the house more often. *(Myra laughs; Kenny, getting stoned, stares at the sock.)*

KENNY. Aunt Myra — what's with the sock?
MYRA. I used to tease her by leaving my socks on her side of the line in our bedroom. Ages ago. Back in Mineola.
KENNY. Oh. *(Suddenly, Myra starts to sniffle.)*
MYRA. Oh man, Kenny — I would do anything if I could just wake up in my bed in Mineola again — and none of this had happened — Hacker, the bank job, the feds, the price on my head — You know what happened to me this week, Kenny? It's like I woke up. I've been walking around in this trance, and all of sudden, when Hacker jumped in the car with the money and his guns, and started screaming, I woke up. I suddenly thought: **"This is real, you asshole, this is happening."**
KENNY. You did it for the Cause, Aunt Myra.
MYRA. Yeah, but which one? First there was the Peace Movement. That's when I first did marijuana. We put daisies in the rifle barrels of the National Guard. I thought if we all just came together, the people, the cops, the narcs, the working class, the bankers — then the war would just stop.
KENNY. That's deep.
MYRA. That's naive, Kenny.
KENNY. Oh. So why'd you do it, Aunt Myra?
MYRA. Well, it's like the story of Jacob and Esau. This cat named Isaac was living in the land of the Chanaanites, which was way out in the suburbs. And he prayed to Yahweh for children to mow his lawn. And God musta heard his prayer, 'cause his wife got buns in the oven. Twin buns. But these twins were as different at birth as Wonderbread and Croissants. There was bad blood between them. No one could clear up the bad blood. One son, Esau, came out all big and hairy and red-necked. The other twin came out sensitive and smooth and small. And this child, Jacob, was a loner in the land of the Chanaanites who were always grunting: "Our Country! Love it or Leave it." And when their time came to kick the bucket, the Chanaanite fathers would give their stash as a blessing to one son, while the other children could go diddle themselves. So the Rich got Richer and the Poor got Fucked Up. And Jacob got wind of this deal coming down. He went out and skinned a sheep and padded himself with its skin so he could pass as Esau. Then Jacob went to Issac's deathbed and said "This is a

hold-up, give me everything you got and nobody will get hurt." And so Jacob got all the loot, and quickly, he rode the hell out of town. He went on a long, long trip far across the borders. And he never came back.

KENNY. What happened to Esau?

MYRA. Who knows? He moved to a nice neighborhood in Great Neck.

KENNY. In a year or so, Aunt Myra, things will cool down and you'll come back.

MYRA. With Tricky Dick in the White House? I don't think so. *(Beat.)* Look, Kenny — it's great to be with you. But it's dangerous, honey. I've got to move out tonight.

KENNY. Aunt Myra? Before we go — can I ask you something? What happened to my mother.

MYRA. I really don't know what goes on in your mother's head, Kenny. She — she said she heard voices. The doctors said shock therapy would be the best thing. So I — so I — well, actually your grandmother and I — we went along and signed the papers.

KENNY. *(Doubt.)* You — you signed the papers?

MYRA. I feel bad about it. I still dream about your mother in the hospital.

KENNY. I'm sure you thought it would help. *(Just then, Myra hears a noise in the hall.)*

MYRA. Shit!! — I knew it! *(Kenny creeps to the door and motions for Myra to be quiet. He cautiously opens the door a crack.)*

KENNY. It's okay. It's the neighbors. It's time for us to go, Aunt Myra.

MYRA. Wait a minute — Kenny — I've been thinking — what if I don't go? What if I decided to surrender to the authorities instead?

KENNY. What?

MYRA. *(Increasingly hysterical.)* What if I say I'm sorry to the security guard, if I say I'm sorry to the bank, if I say I'm sorry to everyone who's ever lived in Mineola — I'll bet I could get some time off the sentence —

KENNY. — Aunt Myra — you're going to make it. I'm going to help you. I'm going with you.

MYRA. Don't be ridiculous, Kenny —

KENNY. I'm not going back to Great Neck! I fucking hate

Great Neck! What is there to do in Great Neck? Argue in school about whether or not we can read CATCHER IN THE RYE?! I missed Woodstock because my bourgeois mother wouldn't let me go! And by the time I get out of high school I'll miss the whole Movement! My mother is a zombie and my father is a joke! *(Myra covers his mouth.)*
MYRA. You're gonna get us both arrested. *(They listen, tense. Then they relax, a little.)*
KENNY. You've got to take me with you!
MYRA. You can't come with me to Canada — all I need is to add federal and international kidnapping charges to my indictment —
KENNY. They won't find us; I'll change my name and my hair and my face and go underground with you — you were supposed to be my real mother; it was all some kind of mistake — she's not my real mother —
MYRA. Shh-shh — Kenny. Listen, in a world of Catholics, everyone's a mistake.
KENNY. You can't do this on your own. You're tired.
MYRA. I know. But — you've got to finish high school.
KENNY. There are high schools in Canada.
MYRA. Kenny! I can't. Don't. I can't think straight.
KENNY. I've got it all planned. The feds will be looking for a single woman terrorist. But — they won't look twice at a mother and her son holding hands as they cross the street.
MYRA. A mother and her son?
KENNY. A mother and her son.
MYRA. Oh — God forgive me. Yes, Kenny Yes! Right now! Kenny! Now! Before I change my mind. We'll go down the fire escape.
KENNY. Yes! *(As they start toward the window, they hear the front door of the apartment building being hammered down —)* You Get Out of Here, Aunt Myra. Go, go, go! I'll try to hold them off — Get Out of Here!
MYRA. Shit! — How the hell did they get the address? — Oh, sshitttt! *(Myra flies across the room and clambers out the window. Kenny looks around for furniture to brace against the door. He sees the single chair and angles it under the knob. There is the sound of a door giving way, and then we hear footsteps running up five flights of stairs. Kenny goes to the window, looks out, hesitates. Just as he decides to climb down,*

35

the front door is burst down by the two federal agents who come into the room with drawn guns. Kenny faces the agents with defiance.)
KENNY. Power to the people! *(Myrna enters, dressed in a London Fog overcoat.)*
MYRNA. Kenneth Ignatious O'Brien Junior! You Are Grounded! *(Kenny slowly faces his mother and raises his hands above his head in surrender.)*

Scene 2

1989

The Corporate Headquarters of Concerned Americans for America. The top floor of an office tower on Madison Avenue. The stage is divided into a very glossy lounge and a sound booth where broadcasting is now in progress. An ON THE AIR sign is lit in the lounge in red.

Back lit, and in shadow, we see a woman seated at the console of radio equipment, wearing headphones, and speaking into a microphone. We hear a voice-over:

"Don't Touch that Dial — right after Rush, right before Paul Harvey — we've got *Talk Back, Get Back,* — *Bite Back:* with M. R. O'Brien, president of Concerned Americans for America. WWKY — Talk Radio — the station you love to hate. Now for the latest hit tunes by Crystal Lewis, Twila Paris and Amy Grant."

As she breaks from her weekly broadcast, the lights come up on the lounge where we can hear M.R. O'Brien on a speaker. Ben, age fourteen, stands in the shadows and waits nervously for the broadcast to end. The Red ON THE AIR sign flashes off. The sound booth door opens, and Myrna O'Brien enters. At first she does not notice Ben.

BEN. Excuse me. Mrs. Myrna O'Brien? *(Myrna looks at Benjamin. Startled, almost by a ghost: He steps into the light.)*
MYRNA. *(Gasping.)* — Oh my God —
BEN. Aunt Myrna? I'm your nephew — Benjamin. Myra's son.
MYRNA. Stand in the light where I can see you. *(Ben steps into the light and raises his hands; he is holding a book.)* What is that you're holding?
BEN. It's your book! *Profiles in Chastity!* I just wanted you to ... autograph it.
MYRNA. You have no idea about the hate mail my show receives. What is it you want from me?
BEN. Just to see you in person.
MYRNA. All right. Mission accomplished?
BEN. *(In a burst.)* I listen to your radio show every week! You're not ashamed of our legacy as Anglo-Saxons. That's what we're taught in school — to be ashamed of being white males. We get hit on the head about the Holocaust and date rape and I hate being in high school! What about all the Germans who died! What about singing Christmas carols! What about roast beef and the Lord's Prayer and standing for the national anthem at football games where there used to be skinny cheerleaders with all-American knockers —
MYRNA. There is a God! *(Myrna laughs.)* Your mother doesn't know you're here?
BEN. No. She — Sarah thinks I'm at the Museum of Natural History for school.
MYRNA. Oh yes — the quaint myth of evolution. Who's Sarah?
BEN. She's my — she's my mother's, uh, significant, um, spousal —
MYRNA. — Oh yes, yes, yes, you needn't go on with all the buzz words. Benjamin has "two mommies." Well. Would you like to sit? *(Ben, nervous and excited, sits.)* What grade are you in, young man?
BEN. Ninth. *(The electronic buzzing echoes under the following.)*
MYRNA. Right after I lost my husband in the accident, I placed Kenny in a military school when he was in ninth grade. I think it's important for young boys to be surrounded by strong men as role models — and then after the academy, he went straight into the Citadel, and then into the service. For the rest of his life Kenny will

have a very straight spine — *(Ben sits up straighter on the sofa.)* Have you thought about what you'd like to be when you grow up?
BEN. I want to be a commentator like you, Aunt Myrna! And a writer. Like you or Barbara Bush. I really liked her book.
MYRNA. Mrs. Bush wrote a lively, engaging account of White House Life from a Dog's perspective. *(Beat.)*
BEN. See, I knew you'd be like this!
MYRNA. Like this?
BEN. You know, warm and really smart — and really, uh, nice.
MYRNA. Instead of?
BEN. Well, you know, Mom thinks that conservatives go around blowing up abortion clinics and stuff — *(Myrna and Ben laugh.)*
MYRNA. Your mother and her imagination. Your mother still works, I gather, for Planned Parenthood of Long Island?
BEN. Yes. I'm afraid she does … Can I — can I ask you something?
MYRNA. Certainly.
BEN. What happened to my mother?
MYRNA. Oh. Well. I'm no expert in these things, of course. You know, your mother as a young woman had quite a "social life" — so why she turned out this way, only scientists in the future will tell us. — Of course, five years in prison, "sharing the soap" didn't help — But I think we choose our way — I think willpower and the right values determine our path.
BEN. So — you don't think um, a way of life —
MYRNA. — Homosexuality is *not* genetic. I do worry about environment but then — see, Benjamin, if we were living in a decent God-fearing state like Virginia, I could sue the state for your custody.
BEN. I mean, Mom and Sarah — do the best they can —
MYRNA. I'm sure they do. Listen, I've had a lot of experience, traveling this great land and all over the world. And let me tell you what I see: I see, sitting before me, a promising young man who — through willpower and thinking — can end up as a leader among men.
BEN. So you think it's a matter of choice?
MYRNA. Some things are *not* a matter of choice. Having a baby is not a choice. It's a gift from God. But who you love, how you live — is a *choice*. We don't talk enough these days about willpower. And young people need to hear that. Every Saturday night, all over

America, husbands and wives *will* themselves to make love to their spouses. They don't want to — but they will themselves to do it. — Do you see what I'm getting at?
BEN. *(Utterly confused.)* I think I do. It would help if I knew who or what my father is ...
MYRNA. Oh yes. Well. Your mother and her ... her "friend" —
BEN. — Sarah?
MYRNA. Yes — I imagine they've told you all about the Facts of Life.
BEN. *(Blushing.)* I know the ... "essentials." They mostly talk about *love* all the time. That it doesn't matter who I love when I grow up — as long as I'm *happy*.
MYRNA. Well, then, you know all about — the egg and the — I hate using the technical words. Like the word that rhymes with "Worm." — See, the left uses technical words to dehumanize what they're doing. They say fetus instead of baby. "Not brought to term" instead of abortion. And they say — the word that rhymes with "worm" —
BEN. — I think I know what you mean —
MYRNA. — Right. I like to call them the Little Guys. I think of the Mystery of Creation as a crowd of Little Guys pushing their way to the front — and each one of us never knows which Little Guy will become King of the Hill. Every Life is a lottery of luck — the luck of the Little Guy. So it doesn't really matter who your father is, Benjamin — he could be Charlie Manson or Henry Mancini. One never knows. We all get the Luck of the Little Guy Draw. *(Beat.)* Now I hope you don't mind me asking you a question —
BEN. You can ask me anything!
MYRNA. See, I've never actually met a living woman who "lives" your mother's "life-style." I heard that a young woman on Senator D'Amato's staff was allegedly a ... a ... *(Myrna hears buzzing.)*
BEN. A lesbian?
MYRNA. Yes. Thank you. And I very much wanted to meet her and ask her questions, but she got fired before I could. So you're the only one I know to ask —
BEN. What do you want to know?
MYRNA. Well: which one is the man?

39

BEN. *(A little horrified.)* The man? It doesn't really work like that ... *(Electronic buzzing.)*
MYRNA. My money's on Myra. I mean, I get scared when I think about — just the thought of kissing a woman makes my stomach heave — doesn't it make you feel a little sea-sick? Well, of course not, you're a young man, it wouldn't make *you* want to heave — you'd have to visualize kissing someone different, like — *(Myrna gets a little dreamy.)* Ohh — Like a young, strapping Olympic athlete with nice, firm pecs —
BEN. Aunt Myrna!
MYRNA. Or a man on a construction crew on a hot summer day who's just removed his undershirt — Do you think that's what they meant when they said one man's meat is another man's poison? — Still, I feel that in my line of work I should really know just what it is they "do" in bed — *(Ben stands in a sweat.)*
BEN. — Um — I have to be going now, Aunt Myrna — I really appreciate your time and — *(Myrna stops him.)*
MYRNA. — Do you see Kenny very often?
BEN. Yes. He comes over for dinner about once a month. Usually with Conchita and the kids.
MYRNA. And every Christmas. Is he — is he all right?
BEN. I think he's fine, Aunt Myrna. I'm really sorry.
MYRNA. Well, he's made his choices. I know he holds me responsible — for sending him away and for your mother's arrest — but if I hadn't taken a firm stand, he was heading for a lifetime of hairdressing or interior decorating. Of course, he would have made good money. But thanks to me, he's a happily married man. Choices!
BEN. I'm sure in time he'll appreciate it —
MYRNA. I wonder.
BEN. And I want to thank you again for letting me meet you —
MYRNA. Oh! My book! Didn't you want my autograph?
BEN. Yes! Please. Very much. *(Myrna takes a pen out of her purse.)*
MYRNA. How shall I inscribe it?
BEN. *(Shyly.)* Well, tomorrow is Sunday — and it's my birthday — so could you please write "Happy Birthday?" *(Myrna writes and hands Ben the book.)*
MYRNA. Happy Birthday! How old are you?

BEN. Fourteen. Tomorrow.
MYRNA. How nice. I'll bet you and your mother and — and your —
BEN. — Sarah —
MYRNA. Yes — are going out for a big Sunday dinner.
BEN. No. Mom's in Chicago. She won't be home until Monday. Some National Board Meeting that she couldn't miss. She said we'll do something next weekend.
MYRNA. A mother should be with her son on his birthday.
BEN. Even if she were home, we'd have to drag her away from the clinic.
MYRNA. On a Sunday? Isn't the clinic closed on a Sunday?
BEN. Yeah. But she works all the time.
MYRNA. Oh. So tomorrow no one's at the — that's too bad. I hope you have a happy birthday, Benjamin.
BEN. Thanks, Aunt Myrna. *(Myrna sees Benjamin to the door.)*
MYRNA. I'm very proud of you. Keep the faith. In another ten years, your mother's "tribe" is going to lose the war. Very soon, if I and my friends can help it, there will come a time when your mother and "Sarah" will have to wear lipstick and heels and try to pass; when they will once again refer to each other as roommates, and where any desire to fulfill their biological destiny will be stopped by the Children's Welfare Agency who will take custody of any offspring they might have. We will never give this country back.
BEN. — Thank you for all you're doing. You're nothing like my mother. *(Ben leaves. Myrna stands in thought. Overlapping music up into Dream Sequence Number Three.)*

Dream Sequence Number Three

The Voice, a disk jockey with a reverb, announces on the air:

Dream Sequence Number Three. Talk Back, Get Back, Bite Back. Myrna O'Brien will take your calls.

A pause. And then seductively, Myrna leans into the microphone:

MYRNA. "Kwaanzaa."
"Felice Navidad."
"Crystal Nacht"
What do these words have in common?
They all evoke a festive time of year. They're impossible to spell, hard to pronounce and ... they're *"foreign."*

But most of all, these words are printed at tax-payer expense in new editions of high school text-books, teaching concepts that the school board calls *"multi-culturalism."*

All-American words have been deleted to make room for these foreign words. Words like: Apple Pie. Norman Rockwell. Spiro Agnew.

Our cultural values are being eradicated to make room for illegal immigrants and militant feminists who want to rewrite the Anglo-Saxon, Christian history of this country.

When tofu-eating-feminazi-fetus-flushing critics scorn us for not offering positive portrayals of women, I Have To Laugh.

What about Mary Todd Lincoln? Julia Dent Grant? Ida Saxton McKinley? Florence Kling Harding? Mamie Dowd Eisenhower? Thelma Ryan Nixon? And countless other women who served under and on top of the great Presidents of this country?

It's time to offer wholesome portraits of American Traditions, and to stop "multi-culturalism" in our schools. I will take your calls. *(Myrna sits in front of a phone panel, with headsets and mike. She looks a bit frightened. Throughout the dream, the sound is distorted, distant and alien. There is a buzz on line one,*

and she answers it:) Talk Back, Get Back, Bite Back — you're on the air: *(And then the echoing sound of Jim Tracey, sobbing:)*
JIM'S VOICE. Myrna? Myrna? Baby? There's — there no one here — for God's sake, Myrna, can't you just talk to me a little — *(We hear Myrna snap a button, disconnecting the caller.)*
MYRNA. Whoopsy. Looks like we've lost caller number one. *(We hear Myrna push another button:)* Get Back — you're on the air: *(Over line two comes the excited voice of a five-year-old girl.)*
CARMELA'S VOICE. Felice Navidad, abuela! Soy Carmela! *(Myrna eagerly rushes to answer in bad Spanish:)*
MYRNA. Felice Navidad, hija! Ha sido una buena chica? Esta tu padre? Is your daddy there? Carmela — Don't hang up on Grandma — No quelga — No quelga — Carmela — put your daddy on the phone — *(There is the sound of Kenny, now grown, picking up the phone:)*
KENNY'S VOICE. Hello?
MYRNA. Kenny? Kenny! Don't hang up — we're on the air — for God's sake, Kenny — can't you just talk to me a little?
KENNY'S VOICE. No-no-no-no-no-no-NO. *(There is the sound of a phone hanging up, and a dial tone. Myrna tries to regain her composure.)*
MYRNA. That was Ken O'Brien Junior, just saying no. *(Another phone call. Myrna stares at it, not wanting to answer, but finally she does:)* Bite Me — *(Myra's high school voice fills the air; the electroshock therapy noise rises as the current passes through Myrna's headset. Breathing and heart beats up.)*
MYRA'S VOICE. *(Urgent whisper.)* Myrna — when the air raid siren comes on, don't hide under your desk. Run down the hallway and out of the building.
MYRNA AND MYRA'S VOICE. **Stay away from the building.**
MYRA'S VOICE. Run to the playground. I'll be waiting.
MYRNA. We can make it home before the blast. Mom says we're to climb into the shelter and lock it, if she and Daddy don't make it home.
MYRA'S VOICE. And after the blast, Mom says not to unlock the door. Not even if she and Daddy beg us too.
MYRNA. There's enough water and canned lima beans to last us six months of nuclear winter.

MYRNA AND MYRA'S VOICE. We'll take care of each other. Okay? *(Just then the air raid siren comes on.)*
MYRA'S VOICE. **Myrna? Myrna? Get to the Door Now.** *(The sound of nuclear holocaust echoes into Scene Six.)*

Scene 3

Lights have come up on an empty parking lot outside Planned Parenthood of Long Island. A Sunday afternoon. Throughout the scene, there is intermittent ticking. Myrna, dressed as Myra in a tailored suit, enters from stage left. She carries a small box, neatly wrapped in brown paper. She looks around her. In a state of excitement, she carefully tucks the box under her arm, and draws out a cellular phone from her hand bag. Myrna dials.

MYRNA. Jerry? Agent Firebird here. *(Myrna stifles a giggle.)* Operation Jane Roe. Not yet. Well, yes, of course I have it. I'm a little scared of putting it down. — Do you know how many speed bumps there are in Nassau County? I haven't had this much fun since Halloween! You should see this wig and how I'm dressed — I'll bet this is exactly how Myra dresses when she networks with NOW members and Emily's List — How much time is on that timer? Oh? Oh. I'd better hustle. — Wait a minute Jerry. There's a woman walking down the street. I'll call you from the car. Over and out. *(Myrna quickly stuffs the receiver back into her purse. Sarah enters from R. and stops.)*
SARAH. — That's the new outfit you bought in Chicago? *(She bursts into laughter.)*
MYRNA. I think it looks ... rather nice.
SARAH. My God — stockings! And you've shaved! That's the kind of Power Suit I always thought your sister would wear —
MYRNA. Thank you.
SARAH. It gives you ... quite a figure. Well — don't I get a kiss? *(Myrna is trying to figure out who this woman is, hoping it's just a friend.)*
MYRNA. Of course. *(Myrna delivers a polite peck on the cheek.)*
SARAH. That's what I get after a week away? I want a real kiss. Oh come on — there's no one around — come here, lover:

(Myrna's eyes bug. Sarah embraces her.)
MYRNA. I — I can't. I'm scared to.
SARAH. You — you don't want to kiss me?
MYRNA. I can't. I'm scared I'll … — give-you-my-cold! I'll give you my cold.
SARAH. — Are we feeling a little shy?
MYRNA. Yes we are.
SARAH. — It's like we're strangers again, isn't it? And we have to get reacquainted all over again. Slowly. Intimately. *(Sarah approaches Myrna.)* Once Benjamin is in bed.
MYRNA. Yes! Benjamin. Where is he?
SARAH. He's been moping all week, thinking you were going to miss his birthday *(Indicating the box.)* — Is that what you got him in Chicago? What is it?
MYRNA. It's a — surprise! *(Before Myrna can stop her, Sarah grabs the box and rattles it to find out what it is.)* No, no, no sweet Jesus — don't do that! *(Sarah stops, stares at Myrna.)* It's — it's very very fragile.
SARAH. Fine — don't tell me. Keep your little secret! — Speaking of secrets —
MYRNA. — Listen — "Sarah" — I need to make a quick call — to see if I can "cancel" something — will you just hold that and *don't move?* *(Myrna rushes off, L.)*
SARAH. *(Calling after:)* Please be here when Ben arrives or you'll ruin the surprise! *(Sarah is left holding the box, waiting. Ticking up. She can feel the box stir, slightly. Her curiosity is getting the better of her. She starts to gently pry at the paper, and starts to remove some tape at one corner in order to peek beneath the wrapping. Just then, Myra rushes in — R., if the actor can manage it. Sarah is almost caught.)*
MYRA. Hello, sweet stuff.
SARAH. Wow, that was quick!
MYRA. Didn't you miss me?
SARAH. You haven't been gone that long. Here, hold this — *(Sarah thrusts the box into Myra's hands.)*
MYRA. What?
SARAH. Ben's Birthday present. Listen — Myra — remember during our last session with Patsy you asked me to tell you about

trouble immediately instead of handling it myself?
MYRA. Benjamin! Don't tell me, he demonstrated for White History Month. *(Sarah takes a book from her shoulder bag, holds it behind her back.)*
SARAH. It's nothing that dramatic, honey. *(Sarah shows Myra the book. Myra is appalled.)*
MYRA. *Profiles in Chastity.* Is this a joke? *(Sarah hands the book to Myra.)*
SARAH. Read the inscription.
MYRA. "Happy Birthday Ben — " Oh. Oh no. He hates me.
SARAH. He doesn't hate you, Myra —
MYRA. *(Waving the book.)* So what is this — love? This is a slap, this is a dagger, this is a bomb —
SARAH. This is why I "handle" things myself.
MYRA. Okay. I'm calm. How do you suggest we handle this?
SARAH. Sometime later this week, why don't you try to have a heart to heart between mother and son?
MYRA. Don't laugh … but he … scares me.
SARAH. He scares you! He's your son, Myra.
MYRA. I know, but … he … scares me. Sometimes I think I've borne my sister's son.
SARAH. Oh no. He's your son. Everything's an absolute with you two — there's no gray.
MYRA. In another ten years, we are going to lose the war. I work my fingers to the bone. Because the day will come that Ben will be left to his own devices by us because we have to work late. He'll borrow our car to study at the library. But instead he'll drive to the lover's lane off the Jericho Turnpike where, because they canceled sex education courses in Nassau County, he'll innocently knock up a girlfriend in the back seat of our car. And when that day comes, thanks to me, he and his girlfriend won't have to make the hard choices between coat hangars and marriage! We will never give this country back!
SARAH. I think we just need to spend more quality time with Ben. *(Sarah takes the book back and puts it in her handbag.)*
MYRA. I hope my next decade is better than this one. Here — hold this. I left something for Ben in my office. *(Myra gives the box back to Sarah and exits.)*

SARAH. — Myra! Don't make any phone calls! Don't read the mail! He'll be here any minute *(Myrna returns, jittery, from L.)*
MYRNA. Give me the box, please. Some things can't be "canceled." *(Myrna makes a grab for the box. Sarah refuses to let go.)*
SARAH. You're not planning to work any more tonight, are you? — I've got to tell you, that Scarsdale Country Club outfit on you is making me hot. I don't know if I can control myself in public —
MYRNA. — Try. Listen, I have to —
SARAH. — Oh, and who made you the prude all of a sudden? Who brought home the leather straps from that little women's boutique last Christmas? *(Myrna turns a shade green.)*
MYRNA. I'm not sure we should get into this in public —
SARAH. — Oh. Right. Be coy. And who was it that broke the straps the very first time we tried — ?
MYRNA. My. That was a treat. Give Me That Box Now. *(Myrna manages to grab the box. She starts to exit.)* I left Ben's ... Card ... behind ... the building. *(Myrna exits left with box. Sarah glances at her watch. Ticking up.)*
SARAH. *(Calling after her.)* I'm here, ready and ... waiting. *(Sarah spruces up the way lesbians do. Myra enters.)*
MYRA. Sarah — we just got an anonymous phone call. A splinter group of Operation Rescue is going to bomb one of our clinics. We have to go on alert.
SARAH. Do you know what day today is?
MYRA. I know it's Ben's birthday.
SARAH. Well?
MYRA. I'll call Chris and ask her to come down so we can go to dinner.
SARAH. Of all days —
MYRA. *(Already exiting.)* — I know. I'll "delegate authority — " Okay? —
SARAH. Patsy's going to be so proud of you! *(Myrna reenters. Ticking up. Sarah blinks at her.)*
MYRNA. Mission Accomplished.
SARAH. You are just buzzing like a little bee today — where's his gift?
MYRNA. I'm giving him something nicer.
SARAH. *(Staring at Myrna's breasts.)* There's something ... dif-

ferent about you ... Did you change your hair?
MYRNA. Yes. No. Let's go. *(Myrna makes a move to go but Sarah grabs her and flirtatiously straightens Myrna's blouse, collar, etc.)*
SARAH. Listen, hon, we're going to a steakhouse Ben wants to go to — so please don't make any cracks about meat, and no cracks about Barbara Bush, and no cracks about Barbara Bush eating meat.
MYRNA. Okay. Let's go.
SARAH. And don't bring up your sister's book. He's just using her to get to you. He'll grow up and see her for what she is. *(Myrna suddenly stops being in such a rush.)*
MYRNA. Oh? Exactly what is she?
SARAH. I'm sure she's just a human being, not some monster who goes around blowing up abortion clinics ... *(Ticking up. Myrna takes Sarah's arm and starts guiding her offstage.)*
MYRNA. Let's go meet Ben, grab a steak, and toast Mrs. Bush — *(As Myrna drags Sarah to exit.)*
SARAH. Boy, this is a switch! I thought I'd have to come in and drag you away from your desk.
MYRNA. From ... my desk? *(A horrible thought crosses Myrna's mind as she realizes Myra is in her office.)* Sarah — this may come out a little strange, but where am I now?
SARAH. Say what?
MYRNA. I have to tell you something.
SARAH. Oh no. You didn't — did you?
MYRNA. Didn't what?
SARAH. Did you — did you sleep with another woman in Chicago?
MYRNA. My God! No!
SARAH. Because you've been acting ... a little strange. You left for Chicago right after our fight and — we have to give the counseling time to work. Every family is dysfunctional when there are teenagers in the house — and I'm trying to listen to my intuition — and I've had this feeling all week that you're in danger. That I'm in danger. And I know you find Patricia Ireland very charismatic. And I know she's more than happily married — but I've been having these images of you casually meeting her after the Contraceptive Technology Panel — a drink, the need to discuss the platform language — it's been

tormenting me. But I would want you to tell me. Did you?
MYRNA. We don't have time for this.
SARAH. *(Exploding.)* That's always the problem. You don't have time for me. You don't have time for Ben. I've had it! I am not moving from this spot until you show me how much you love me. I want a kiss.
MYRNA. Now?
SARAH. Now! *(Myrna crosses herself, goes to Sarah. They kiss. Deeply. Just then Ben enters.)*
BEN. Aunt Myrna? What are you doing ? *(Sarah turns, horrified, and stares at Myrna.)*
MYRNA. Benjamin. I am … so sorry. You told me — your mother was in Chicago. Or I would never have —
BEN. What's that ticking?
MYRNA. Please. You've got to —
BEN. — Where's Mom? *(Ben looks at Myrna with an awful suspicion. Ticking loud.)*
MYRNA. Please both of you — stay calm.
BEN. Mom? Mom? — *(Ben runs offstage to the building.)*
MYRNA. No! Ben!
SARAH. *(Calling after him.)* Ben!
MYRNA. **Stay away from the building.**
SARAH. — Oh My God. You're bombing the building. *(Sarah runs after Ben. Myrna turns to leave, but is stopped by the sound of amplified breathing and the echo of Myra's childhood voice:)*
MYRA'S VOICE. **Myrna? Myrna?** *(The sound of amplified gulping and soft heart beats. Myrna concentrates in a trance:)*
MYRNA. **Myra. Get to the *door* NOW.** *(She is answered by the amplified sound of heart beating louder.)* Myra! *(As Myrna runs towards the clinic we hear her voice reverberating in an echo of "Myra get to the door NOW." A beat later, as the lights dim, we hear the sound of a loud explosion.)*

Dream Sequence Number Four

The Voice narrates:

Dream Sequence Number Four. Myra in Mineola dreaming of Myrna in Mineola dreaming of Myra. Together Again.

Lights start to come up. We see Myra in her nightgown. Her bed is behind her. The sound of amplified breathing and heartbeats. The lights dissolve into a dark and stormy night. Thunder, lightning. Myra dreams she is age sixteen back in her bedroom in Mineola. There is a violent clap of thunder.

MYRA. That last one was awfully close. Are you asleep? ... Can I get into your bed until the storm passes? *(Another crash, closer. Myra, scared, tiptoes to an imaginary line.)* I'm going to cross over the line, okay? The line dividing your half from mine? I know we're not supposed to cross it except in case of fire or nuclear emergencies but — *(A terrific crash. Myra shivers.)* It's getting closer. *(No response. Thunder rumbles.)* Can't you just talk to me a little? *(Pause. Myra's a little closer to crying. The sound of an amplified heart beating More lightning.)* You're scaring me! *(The heart beats faster; Myra fights for a little control.)* ... I can hear your heart beating. I know you're not asleep. I just want to say ... I'm sorry. Okay? I'm sorry ... for everything. *(No answer; but we can feel the other sister listening. Myra summons up all of her courage, and in a whisper:)* And I really wish ... I wish we could be closer. *(An even louder crash and flash of lightning: Myrna rises from the bed during the lightning bolt — the twins reach for each other, calling to each other:)*
MYRA: **Myrna!** MYRNA. **Myra!**

Lights change. We see the double bed that Myra shares with Sarah in Mineola. Myra sits up remembering the dream. There is the sound of thunder moving off in the distance. Sarah wakes up, turns on the light.

SARAH. Myra? Honey? You okay? *(A beat.)* Were you having a bad dream?
MYRA. I don't remember. *(Myra hardens herself against her dream.)* That crazy, murdering bitch almost blew Ben, you, and me up to pieces.
SARAH. We almost blew up together, just like any other happy nuclear family. *(Beat. Sarah holds out her arms.)* We're not going to think about it. Come here. Come on. I'll just hold you. Until you can sleep. Okay? *(Myra nods, and settles in on Sarah's shoulder. Beat.)*
MYRA. Sarah? Do you think Myrna will go to jail?
SARAH. I'm sure she's got very good lawyers.
MYRA. Jail wasn't so bad. I was terrified at first. But then it turned out to be just like Detention Hall at Mineola High. And then I noticed there were no mirrors in maximum security. For the first time in my life, I didn't have to see my sister's face. *(Beat.)* Sarah? It wasn't just luck. That I happened to leave my office seconds before the blast. I heard … a voice. Like the voice on the intercom. It said: Get to the Door Now.
SARAH. You hear voices.
MYRA. Sometimes. I think it's my sister's voice. But sometimes I worry that it could be mine. We sound the same.
SARAH. *(Holding Myra tighter.)* You're in your own home in Mineola, in your own bed beside me, and Ben is asleep down the hall. She can't get you here. Okay? Think you can sleep?
MYRA. Yes. *(Sarah kisses Myra and settles down in bed next to her.)* Good night. *(Sarah begins to drift.)*
SARAH. Sleep tight, honey. *(The light fades more; Myra sits in bed, unable to sleep. A pause, and then, in the darkening room, we hear a Voice call:)* **Sweet dreams.** *The lights change more. A*

teenage Myrna rises from the bed on the other side of Sarah. Myrna and Myra stare at each other. Then they reach for each other across the sleeping Sarah. Just as they touch, the beds pull apart into two twin islands; the twins still reach for each other as the distance between them increases. The lights fade to Blackout and End of Play.)

PROPERTY LIST

Pipe (JIM)
Cigarette, lit (MYRA)
Gum (MYRA)
Car keys (JIM)
Sock (MYRNA, MYRA)
Transistor radio (KENNY)
2 Styrofoam cups (FBI MEN)
Money (JIM)
Bank literature (FBI MEN)
Folded slip of paper (MYRNA)
Bulging envelope with money (MYRNA)
Roll of toilet paper (MYRA)
Can of Coca-Cola (MYRA)
Pill (MYRA)
Joint (MYRA)
Book (BEN)
Purse (MYRNA) with:
    pen
    cell phone
Headset (MYRNA)
Microphone (MYRNA)
Small box wrapped in brown paper (MYRNA)
Shoulder bag with book (SARAH)

SOUND EFFECTS

Window pried open
Thud
Thump
Automobile starting up, revved, put into reverse
Automobile screeching away
Electric shock therapy buzzing
Amplified breathing
Amplified beating heart
Phone hang up
Dial tone
Air raid siren
Nuclear holocaust explosion
Ticking
Loud explosion
Loud thunder
Thunder moving away

NEW PLAYS

★ **THE CIDER HOUSE RULES, PARTS 1 & 2 by Peter Parnell, adapted from the novel by John Irving.** Spanning eight decades of American life, this adaptation from the Irving novel tells the story of Dr. Wilbur Larch, founder of the St. Cloud's, Maine orphanage and hospital, and of the complex father-son relationship he develops with the young orphan Homer Wells. "...luxurious digressions, confident pacing...an enterprise of scope and vigor..." *–NY Times*. "...The fact that I can't wait to see Part 2 only begins to suggest just how good it is..." *–NY Daily News*. "...engrossing...an odyssey that has only one major shortcoming: It comes to an end." *–Seattle Times*. "...outstanding...captures the humor, the humility...of Irving's 588-page novel..." *–Seattle Post-Intelligencer*. [9M, 10W, doubling, flexible casting] PART 1 ISBN: 0-8222-1725-2 PART 2 ISBN: 0-8222-1726-0

★ **TEN UNKNOWNS by Jon Robin Baitz.** An iconoclastic American painter in his seventies has his life turned upside down by an art dealer and his ex-boyfriend. "...breadth and complexity...a sweet and delicate harmony rises from the four cast members...Mr. Baitz is without peer among his contemporaries in creating dialogue that spontaneously conveys a character's social context and moral limitations..." *–NY Times*. "...darkly funny, brilliantly desperate comedy...TEN UNKNOWNS vibrates with vital voices." *–NY Post*. [3M, 1W] ISBN: 0-8222-1826-7

★ **BOOK OF DAYS by Lanford Wilson.** A small-town actress playing St. Joan struggles to expose a murder. "...[Wilson's] best work since *Fifth of July*...An intriguing, prismatic and thoroughly engrossing depiction of contemporary small-town life with a murder mystery at its core...a splendid evening of theater..." *–Variety*. "...fascinating...a densely populated, unpredictable little world." *–St. Louis Post-Dispatch*. [6M, 5W] ISBN: 0-8222-1767-8

★ **THE SYRINGA TREE by Pamela Gien.** Winner of the 2001 Obie Award. A breathtakingly beautiful tale of growing up white in apartheid South Africa. "Instantly engaging, exotic, complex, deeply shocking...a thoroughly persuasive transport to a time and a place...stun[s] with the power of a gut punch..." *–NY Times*. "Astonishing...affecting ...[with] a dramatic and heartbreaking conclusion...A deceptive sweet simplicity haunts THE SYRINGA TREE..." *–A.P.* [1W (or flexible cast)] ISBN: 0-8222-1792-9

★ **COYOTE ON A FENCE by Bruce Graham.** An emotionally riveting look at capital punishment. "The language is as precise as it is profane, provoking both troubling thought and the occasional cheerful laugh...will change you a little before it lets go of you." *–Cincinnati CityBeat*. "...excellent theater in every way..." *–Philadelphia City Paper*. [3M, 1W] ISBN: 0-8222-1738-4.

★ **THE PLAY ABOUT THE BABY by Edward Albee.** Concerns a young couple who have just had a baby and the strange turn of events that transpire when they are visited by an older man and woman. "An invaluable self-portrait of sorts from one of the few genuinely great living American dramatists...rockets into that special corner of theater heaven where words shoot off like fireworks into dazzling patterns and hues." *–NY Times*. "An exhilarating, wicked...emotional terrorism." *–NY Newsday*. [2M, 2W] ISBN: 0-8222-1814-3

★ **FORCE CONTINUUM by Kia Corthron.** Tensions among black and white police officers and the neighborhoods they serve form the backdrop of this discomfiting look at life in the inner city. "The creator of this intense...new play is a singular voice among American playwrights...exceptionally eloquent..." *–NY Times*. "...a rich subject and a wise attitude." *–NY Post*. [6M, 2W, 1 boy] ISBN: 0-8222-1817-8

DRAMATISTS PLAY SERVICE, INC.
440 Park Avenue South, New York, NY 10016 212-683-8960 Fax 212-213-1539
postmaster@dramatists.com   www.dramatists.com